CONTENTS

D0189070

PART ONE
INTRODUCTION

PART TWO
PLOT AND ACTION

PART THREE
CHARACTERS

PART FOUR
KEY CONTEXTS AND THEMES

PART FIVE
LANGUAGE AND STRUCTURE

PART SIX
GRADE BOOSTER

Study and revision advice

There are two main stages to your reading and work on *Of Mice and Men*. First, the study of the book as you read it. Second, your preparation or revision for exam or controlled assessment. These top tips will help you with both.

 READING AND STUDYING THE NOVEL – DEVELOP INDEPENDENCE!

- Try to engage and respond personally to the characters, ideas and story – not just for your enjoyment, but also because it helps you develop your own **independent ideas** and **thoughts** about *Of Mice and Men*. This is something that examiners are very keen to see.

- **Talk** about the text with friends and family; ask questions in class; put forward your own viewpoint – and, if time, **read around** the text to find out about life in America in the 1930s.

- Take time to **consider** and **reflect** on the **key elements** of the novel; keep your own notes, mind-maps, diagrams, scribbled jottings about the characters and how you respond to them; follow the story as it progresses (what do you think might happen?); discuss the main themes and ideas (what do *you* think it is about? Dreams? Friendship? Loneliness?); pick out language that impresses you or makes an **impact**, and so on.

- Treat your studying **creatively**. When you write essays or give talks about the book make your responses creative. Think about using really clear ways of explaining yourself, use unusual **quotations**, well-chosen **vocabulary**, and try powerful, persuasive ways of beginning or ending what you say or write.

 REVISION – DEVELOP ROUTINES AND PLANS!

- **Good revision** comes from **good planning**. Find out when your exam or controlled assessment is and then plan to look at key aspects of *Of Mice and Men* on different days or times during your revision period. You could use these Notes – see 'How can these Notes help me' – and add dates or times when you are going to cover a particular topic.

- Use **different ways** of **revising**. Sometimes talking about the text and what you know/don't know with a friend or member of the family can help; other times, filling a sheet of A4 with all your ideas in different colour pens about a character, for example LENNIE, can make ideas come alive; other times, making short lists of quotations to learn, or numbering events in the plot can assist you.

- **Practise plans** and **essays**. As you get nearer the 'day', start by looking at essay questions and writing short bulleted plans. Do several plans (you don't have to write the whole essay); then take those plans and add details to them (quotations, linked ideas). Finally, using the advice in **Part Six: Grade Booster**, write some practice essays and then check them out against the advice we have provided.

 **EXAMINER'S TIP**

Prepare for the exam or controlled assessment! Whatever you need to bring, make sure you have it with you – books, if you are allowed, pens, pencils – and that you turn up on time.

Introducing *Of Mice and Men*

SETTING

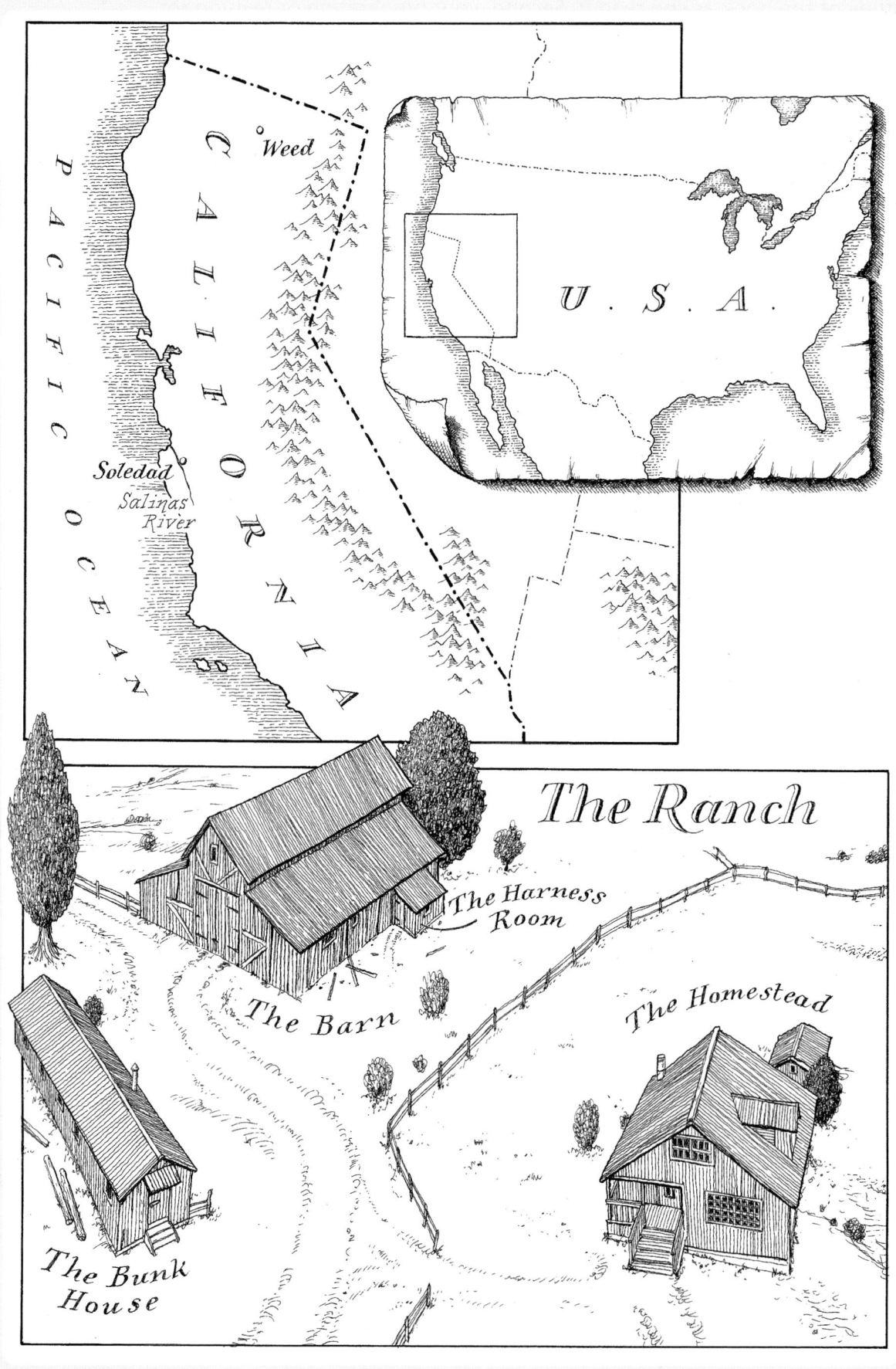

CHARACTERS: WHO'S WHO

GEORGE and LENNIE
Two migrant workers.

CANDY and his DOG
An old man who cleans the ranch, and his dog.

SLIM
Head of one of the 'grain teams'.

CARLSON and WHIT
- Workers on the Ranch.

CROOKS
A stable hand.

CURLEY and CURLEY'S WIFE
The boss's son (an ex-boxer) and his new wife.

THE BOSS
The man in charge of the ranch.

JOHN STEINBECK: AUTHOR AND CONTEXT

1902 John Ernst Steinbeck born 27 February in Salinas, California

1917 USA enters First World War

1925 Steinbeck leaves university without a degree and goes to New York

1929 'Great Crash' on Wall Street, start of the Great Depression; Steinbeck publishes his first novel, *Cup of Gold*

1930 Steinbeck marries Carol Henning

1937 *Of Mice and Men* published

1939–45 Second World War

1940 Steinbeck's first marriage breaks up; *Grapes of Wrath* wins Pulitzer Prize

1962 Steinbeck awarded the Nobel Prize for Literature

1968 Steinbeck dies of heart disease

Plot summary: What happens in *Of Mice and Men*?

REVISION ACTIVITY

- Go through the summary boxes below and **highlight** what you think is the **key moment** in each section.

- Then find each moment in the **text** and **reread** it. Write down **two reasons** why you think each moment is so **important**.

SECTION ONE

- George and Lennie, having walked a long way, stop at a pool by the Salinas River.

- They are off to take up work at a nearby ranch.

- They have had to leave their previous work for some, as yet to be explained, reason to do with Lennie.

- It is clear that Lennie is slow to understand. He has been keeping a dead mouse to 'pet'. George makes him get rid of it.

- We learn that they left Weed because Lennie had touched a girl's dress, she'd shouted out, and they'd had to hide in a ditch to escape angry townsfolk.

- George tells Lennie a story he has obviously told before about how one day they plan to have their own little farm.

- George makes Lennie promise to meet him at the pool if there's trouble.

SECTION TWO

- George and Lennie start work at the farm.

- They meet the other ranch hands, the boss's aggressive son Curley, and Curley's wife who comes into the bunk house and flirts with them.

- Lennie is attracted to Curley's wife and George is worried.

- George makes Lennie promise to meet him by the pool if there is any trouble.

- They also meet Slim, in charge of the horses, who is a man with natural authority.

SECTION THREE

George reveals to Slim why they were 'run out' of Weed.

Slim gives Lennie a puppy from his own dog's litter.

Carlson, a farm hand, convinces Candy, an old man who cleans up around the farm, to let his aged dog be shot.

Candy overhears George and Lennie's plan for their own farm and offers to put in half the money if they will let him join them.

Curley comes in and starts a fight with Lennie, hitting him until George tells Lennie to fight back. Lennie breaks Curley's hand.

Slim makes Curley say that his hand was injured in an accident.

SECTION FOUR

- While the other ranch hands go out to the local town Lennie enters the hut of Crooks, a crippled stable hand.

- Candy also appears and they tell Crooks about their dream for the farm.

- They are interrupted by Curley's wife who laughs at them and threatens Crooks with a charge of rape when he tells her to leave.

- Later, Lennie accidentally kills the pup he has been given, not knowing his own strength.

SECTION FIVE

Lennie tries to bury the puppy in the straw in the barn.

Curley's wife comes in and they talk, and she asks him to stroke her hair.

She panics when she feels Lennie's strength, and in grabbing her he breaks her neck by accident.

When the body is found it is obvious Lennie is the killer.

A hunt is started for him, with Curley keen to be the one who shoots Lennie.

SECTION SIX

- George realises Lennie could not bear life in prison, and also can't stand the thought of him being lynched by Curley and the others.

- George finds Lennie by the pool where they had agreed to meet if there was trouble.

- He talks to Lennie about their dream farm, and then shoots him just before the others arrive.

- Slim comforts George and tells him he had no choice.

Section One: Moving on

SUMMARY

1. The setting of the Salinas River, 'south of Soledad', is introduced.

2. Lennie and George arrive by a pool, and Lennie drinks from the water, 'like a horse'. He is a huge man and George is small.

3. Lennie has been carrying a dead mouse to 'pet', but George takes it from him and throws it away.

4. We find out that they have come from a town in the north, Weed, and are going to a ranch for work. George tells Lennie not to speak to the boss when they get there, or he'll know how 'crazy' Lennie is.

5. When Lennie comes back from collecting wood for the fire, he has retrieved the dead mouse, but George realises and takes it from him a second time.

6. We find out more about George and how he looks after Lennie. We also learn the reason why they had to leave Weed – because Lennie touched a girl's dress and she screamed, thinking she was being attacked.

7. Lennie asks George to tell him about the farm they plan to have one day.

8. George makes Lennie promise that if there's any future trouble he'll come back to the same pool and wait for George until he arrives.

CHECKPOINT 1

Which animals are described in the opening chapter?

WHY IS THIS SECTION IMPORTANT?

A It establishes the **setting**.
B We are introduced to the **two main characters**, Lennie and George.
C Their **relationship** is made clear.
D We find out **what has happened previously** in Weed (the reason they are here now), and are told **where they are going next**.
E It provides initial **clues** about **key ideas**, **themes** and **events** which will come up again as the book progresses.

THE SETTING: STILL LIFE, HOT NIGHT

The book opens with a varied and colourful description of the rural Californian setting, south of Soledad by the Salinas River, in particular a 'narrow pool' by which Lennie and George eventually make camp. Like a stage-set, the place seems to be waiting for their arrival, and Steinbeck uses vivid **images** to create the warm, dry evening.

The rabbits Steinbeck describes will come to have greater significance as the novel progresses. The **simile** he uses to describe them as 'sculptured stones' adds to the mythic or timeless feel. Later Steinbeck uses the **present tense**, which further contributes to the timelessness, but also suggests this is a real place that still survives today.

The detailed snapshot of nature tells us that many other men have stopped there, and could imply George and Lennie are small, unimportant figures in the world.

EXAMINER'S TIP

Read your exam question carefully. If it's about the **culture** of *Of Mice and Men* – the US background, farm, working life – stick to those elements.

KEY QUOTE

'On the sand-banks the rabbits sat as quietly as little gray, sculptured stones.' (p. 2)

LENNIE AND GEORGE: FRIENDS AND FOES?

Lennie and George's introduction emphasises their similarity at first – 'both' wear the same denim clothing and black hats. But George is small and has 'defined' features. Lennie is huge, rather 'shapeless' and bear-like.

Steinbeck's use of **metaphor** makes Lennie's bear-like qualities clear, but his delight in causing ripples also implies his simple-minded, child-like nature.

George, for his part, is presented as both irritated and angered by Lennie's simplicity, but feels responsible for him.

The 'bad things' and 'hot water' Lennie gets George into are revealed – he touched the girl's dress in Weed. This, along with Lennie's fixation with things to pet' **foreshadow** events later in the story. However, their closeness is revealed by their shared enjoyment of the dream of owning a farm.

EXAMINER'S TIP: WRITING ABOUT LENNIE'S DREAM

This section is very important. It not only establishes the closeness of Lennie and George – the 'farm speech' has obviously been recited before – but makes us sympathetic to their simple ambition. Their dream is to have a small farm to 'live off the fatta the lan!' as Lennie says. Lennie's response to it is like a small child being told a favourite bedtime story.

The dream of the farm seems very much Lennie's fantasy here, but later, when we meet Candy, the old man at the ranch, it suddenly seems to become a reality. The **key theme** of **dreams and hopes** is therefore placed right at the start of the novel.

? **DID YOU KNOW**

The fact that the water Lennie drinks from at the start of the novel is described by George as 'kinda scummy' (p. 5) is said by some critics to warn us of an unhappy ending.

KEY QUOTE

'Lennie dabbled his big paw in the water and wiggled his fingers so the water arose in little splashes' (p. 3)

★ GRADE BOOSTER

Think originally! For example, George seems decent, but you could argue he has an unpleasant side, criticising Lennie and ordering him around.

Section Two: Rising tensions

SUMMARY

CHECKPOINT 2

What do we learn about the bunk house from the opening paragraph of this section?

1. George and Lennie have arrived at the ranch and are shown the bunk house by the 'old swamper' (cleaner) Candy, who has an old dog.

2. George worries that the previous occupant of his bunk had lice.

3. The boss is talked about – 'a pretty nice fella' – and the stable-hand Crooks. The boss meets George and Lennie.

4. Curley, the boss's son, comes into the bunk house, and picks on Lennie, seeming to want a fight. Curley is 'pretty handy. He done quite a bit in the ring'. He also 'hates big guys'.

5. Curley's wife visits the bunk house, and flirts with the men.

6. George becomes even more worried. Curley frightens George – 'I hate that kind of guy'.

7. George reminds Lennie he is to go to the pool if there is 'trouble'.

8. Slim, the 'jerk line skinner' and unofficial leader of the ranch hands, meets George and Lennie. He wins George's confidence with his natural authority and 'dignity'.

9. Slim offers to give Lennie one of the pups recently born to his dog.

WHY IS THIS SECTION IMPORTANT?

A It **introduces** us to **the bunk house**, the home of the ranch hands and setting for much of the novel.

B It **introduces** us to some of the **main characters** at the ranch.

C Curley is clearly identified as a **threat** to **Lennie and George**, as is **his wife**.

D We are given clear hints that there is **trouble ahead**.

THE CHARACTERS: HEROES AND VILLAINS

EXAMINER'S TIP

You will be given marks for showing you know what a character is like. You can gain even more marks if you show you know how Steinbeck has given the reader the information. In Slim's case we are told what his character is. With Candy, Steinbeck uses a different method. Candy's dog – old, worn out – actually sums up Candy as well. What other ways does Steinbeck use to tell us about his characters?

Steinbeck shows us real people, good and bad, and this mixture helps to persuade u that the world he shows us in *Of Mice and Men* is also real. Steinbeck does not fall i to the trap of describing all those in power as evil. The Boss is a decent man, although he has a temper.

Steinbeck uses **dialogue** to create characterisation. Each character has their own way of speaking – look at sentence length, use of slang, repetition and accents. The characters are all ranch hands or work on the same farm, but immediately we meet them we see how different they are, from the dignity of Slim to the anger of Curley.

Steinbeck can show us characters with serious weaknesses (Curley, Curley's wife) and with great strengths (George, Slim), but his real interest is in people who are the oppressed and the weak, yearning and failing to take control of their lives: George, Lennie and Candy.

 DID YOU KNOW

Blue jeans, which are now designer fashion items, were developed in America as cheap and durable work trousers.

LONELINESS

George and Lennie interest Slim because 'you guys travel around together', and this clearly unusual. As the novel goes on we see more and more how lonely the life of the migrant, wandering worker is. Candy is desperately alone, except for his dog.

re Curley and his wife lonely? There's certainly no friendship in their marriage. his sense of loneliness – summed up by Slim when he says 'Maybe ever'body in the whole damned world is scared of each other' – helps us realise how special the iendship is between George and Lennie.

KEY QUOTE

'We kinda look after each other.' (p. 38)

EXAMINER'S TIP: WRITING ABOUT SLIM

Steinbeck makes it clear that Slim is a hero, 'the prince of the ranch'. He commands everyone's respect, and is the only character Steinbeck uses a whole paragraph to praise.

Does Steinbeck overdo the hero worship? Steinbeck has been accused of admiring physical skills in men at the expense of intellectual or thinking skills. Yet the respect Slim receives is as much the result of his personality as his ability to 'kill a fly on the wheeler's butt with a bull whip without touching the mule'.

Is there a comparison here with the modern criticism that we make heroes out of rock stars or sportsmen, when their talents may not match up the praise and hero-worship we heap on them?

GRADE BOOSTER

Ask yourself if Slim really is as perfect as Steinbeck makes him out to be.

Section Three: The dawn of hope

SUMMARY

1 Slim gives one of the puppies his dog has had to Lennie.

2 Slim and George talk about Lennie, and George explains that he took over caring for Lennie when Lennie's Aunt Clara died – 'Got kinda used to each other after a while'.

3 George explains why they were 'run out' of Weed, reassures Slim that Lennie did not rape the girl and patiently makes Lennie put the pup back with its mother when he tries to smuggle it into the bunk house.

4 Carlson persuades a reluctant Candy to let him shoot Candy's old dog. He will use the Luger pistol he owns –'The way I'd shoot him, he wouldn't feel nothing'.

5 Whit shows Slim a letter written to a magazine of cowboy stories by a hand who once worked on the ranch.

6 Whit asks George to join the other ranch hands in a visit the next night to the local town and brothel.

7 Curley bursts in, looking for his wife, and argues over her with Slim.

8 George and Lennie discuss their dream – 'We could live offa the fatta the lan'' – and Candy asks to buy himself in with money he has saved.

9 Curley picks a fight with Lennie, who does not fight back until George orders Lennie to do so. Lennie crushes Curley's hand – 'Looks to me like ever' bone in his han' is bust'.

10 Slim protects Lennie from blame for the injury to Curley, and makes Curley say it was an accident with a machine that caused the injury.

WHY IS THIS SECTION IMPORTANT?

A It makes us think for a brief moment that **George and Lennie's dream** might **actually happen**: Candy clearly does have the money necessary. Then the dream is **shattered** by Curley, showing that in real-life dreams rarely come true.

B It explains in more detail the **relationship** between George and Lennie, and reinforces the **importance of loneliness** in the novel.

C The mention of the cowboy magazine the ranch hands pretend to scorn but secretly admire is introduced. It is **another dream**, like Lennie and George's – something unreal but something which helps make life bearable.

D Lennie's pathetic plea to George after he has crushed Curley's hand – 'I din't mean no harm, George' – sums up **Lennie**.

E The shooting of Candy's dog shows us **the cruelty of the world** portrayed in the novel. It prepares us for the shooting of Lennie.

? **DID YOU KNOW**

When Steinbeck was writing *East of Eden* in his special writing room in his New York house, he also built a boat there on a carpenter's work bench he had had installed.

THE WILD WEST?

The ranch hands outwardly scorn the Wild West magazines that they buy, but secretly they enjoy the romantic, glamorous view that the magazines give of cowboys and, by association, of ranch hands.

The magazines show the workers how they would like to be. This is another dream, similar to that of George and Lennie. It will never be real, but it is necessary for surviving in the real world.

SATURDAY NIGHT VISITS

George and Whit talk about Susy's, a brothel where the men go on Saturday nights.

Note how delicately Steinbeck handles the discussion. It could easily become coarse and obscene. In Steinbeck's hands it becomes natural, a normal part of a man's life. This is not to justify the exploitation of prostitutes, but it shows how Steinbeck refuses to impose a politically correct agenda onto his writing.

Steinbeck is concerned to reveal what the men think and feel, not to prove a point about what they ought to think. He tries to show life as it is, and as how it looks from inside the minds of his **characters**.

EXAMINER'S TIP: WRITING ABOUT LIGHT

Note the importance that light plays in Steinbeck's description. The section starts with a description of light – 'Although there was evening brightness showing through the windows of the bunk house, inside it was dusk'.

Much of the atmosphere in the discussion between Slim and George is created by the pool of light that the shaded lamp throws in the bunk house. Steinbeck uses light as it is used on stage – to create mood and atmosphere. The effect in this case is to suggest intimacy and cosiness.

KEY QUOTE

'Instantly the table was brilliant with light' (p. 42)

Section Four: Death on the farm

SUMMARY

1. Lennie wanders into the harness room where Crooks, the black stable hand – 'a proud, aloof man' – lives. George and the other hands are out on the town.

2. Crooks talks to Lennie.

3. Crooks teases Lennie that George might leave him, and is frightened by Lennie's response.

4. Candy joins them and Crooks finds himself half believing that the dream of the small farm might actually happen.

5. Curley's wife comes in, and when Crooks shows his anger at her she threatens to accuse him of rape and have him lynched.

WHY IS THIS SECTION IMPORTANT?

A The section is almost **a rest period before the final climax**. Many authors step down the tension a little before a major climax, almost as if to give the reader a break before a very demanding section.

B The section introduces the issue of **racial prejudice**.

C Lennie's anger at Crooks warns us again that **Lennie can be dangerous**.

D The **harsh injustice of the world** is shown by the ease with which Curley's wife can humiliate Crooks.

E **Loneliness** is again emphasised.

CROOKS: PREJUDICE OR LONELINESS?

Crooks is a bitter, cynical person. Does his bitterness come from his being badly treated? Steinbeck draws the reader's attention to how few rights black people had He reveals that Crooks could be lynched, without a trial, if Curley's wife so much as accuses him of trying to rape her.

Perhaps Crooks's bitterness is also due to his being disabled – he is continually rubbing his injured back with liniment.

Above all, Crooks is shown as a lonely man, isolated from the others by his race and his disability. Steinbeck seems at least as interested in loneliness as he is in racial prejudice. He is also interested in the effects of prejudice against those of different races or who have physical problems.

Crooks's room is important in the novel. He guards it fiercely, showing how isolated and alone a black man is on a ranch where all the other people are white. His room is both a symbol of Crooks as someone different and isolated from the others, and a private place where he can be himself. It is also a working room, its contents showing some of the skills needed to 'work' a ranch at that time.

KEY QUOTE

'Everybody wants a little bit of land, not much. Jus' som'thin' that was his.' (p. 83)

CHECKPOINT 3

How many people are left on the ranch on the night covered in this section?

**EXAMINER'S TIP**

It's a good idea to comment on the colloquial speech the characters use, but be careful to write your essays in formal English.

CURLEY'S WIFE: A COMPLEX CHARACTER

[Th]e easy thing to do is to criticise Curley's wife. She is a flirt, who likes attracting [m]en's attention and seems to enjoy the trouble she creates. She glories in the power [s]he has over Crooks, a power she has not earned.

[A]t the same times, she is also a victim. There is no love between her and Curley. He [h]as gone to a brothel. There is nothing for her to do on the ranch – 'Think I don't [li]ke to talk to somebody ever' once in a while? Think I like to stick in that house alla [t]ime?'

[L]oneliness does not excuse Curley's wife, but it does help both to explain her and to [s]uggest she is, like Lennie, a victim of a cruel world.

EXAMINER'S TIP: WRITING ABOUT PRIDE AND PREJUDICE

This section is important for the theme of shattered dreams. Crooks is described as 'proud and aloof'. A good question to ask is how someone who has so little can still be proud. Note that Crooks initially tries to buy into the dream of the small farm, but then withdraws his request after Curley's wife humiliates him. Crooks's pride comes from the fact that he has no dreams, and no illusions about life being fair. This gives him the strength to be proud. As he has no hopes, it is almost as if no one can hurt him.

★ **GRADE BOOSTER**

Look at how 'theatrical' this section is, very like a play. It takes place in one room, like a stage set, characters walk in and out as they would in a play and the action is pushed forward by **dialogue**, as it would be in a play.

? DID YOU KNOW

Steinbeck was so fed up with people pestering him that he equipped a station wagon as a mobile study so that he could 'get away from it all' to write.

KEY QUOTE

'Crooks had retired in to the terrible protective dignity of the negro.' (p. 86)

Section Five: Murder by mistake

SUMMARY

1. Lennie has killed the puppy Slim gave him – 'Why do you got to get killed? You ain't so little as mice.'

2. He tries to bury it secretly in the barn.

3. Curley's wife enters and talks to Lennie about her dislike of Curley and her wish to be a movie star.

4. She invites Lennie to stroke her hair, but panics when she feels his strength.

5. Lennie panics, tries to quieten her and then gets angry and shakes her to death.

6. A manhunt is organised to find Lennie, who has fled.

7. George implies to Candy that the dream of a small farm is over – 'I think I knowed we'd never do her.'

KEY QUOTE

'She was very pretty and simple, and her face was sweet and young.' (p. 101)

WHY IS THIS SECTION IMPORTANT?

A It seals **Lennie's fate**.
B It shows the **sad loneliness** of Curley's wife, as well as her negative affect on others.
C It suggests that **the dream of the farm** will **die with Lennie**.

PORTRAYING MEN AND WOMEN

EXAMINER'S TIP

It is important to respond individually to the text and draw links with modern racism and discrimination, but remember the key thing is to write about Steinbeck's own views.

Some feminists argue that Steinbeck encourages old-fashioned stereotypical images of women. They argue that Steinbeck sees the use of prostitutes as a man's right, and that the only woman who appears in the novel is a passive victim, a threat to men and someone described simply in terms of her sexuality.

Yet the men in the novel are also frequently imperfect, and Steinbeck has sympathy for Curley's wife: she is portrayed as a pathetic figure, with her own unrealisable dream, married to a man she hates and with nothing to distract her from her unhappy marriage. In her own way, perhaps she is as much of a victim as Lennie.

In basing his novel largely round a group of men and what we might see nowadays as 'macho' values, Steinbeck is writing in a firmly American tradition – the leading novelist of which is Ernest Hemingway. Steinbeck's concentration on male figures in *Of Mice and Men* allows him to examine a theme more closely studied in *The Grapes of Wrath*: in the America of the 1930s, men are in charge. Yet both novels show how little anyone, male or female, is actually in control of their lives.

GRADE BOOSTER

Look at Steinbeck's choice of language. Are the lines, 'As happens sometimes, a moment settled and hovered ... much, much more than a moment' (p. 101) too 'poetic', too rich, in comparison with the rather objective, detached style Steinbeck adopts elsewhere?

DREAMS AND REALITY

George seems to tell Candy that their deal to buy a small farm is over – 'I think I knowed we'd never do her.' In some way this has to mean that Lennie was as important in the dream as the money.

One answer is that George knew all along this was just a dream, an idea that brought comfort but which he knew would never happen.

It could also mean that George wanted the farm because it was the only way to find peace for Lennie, rather than something George wanted to do.

Most of all it shows that humans have a dream world where good things happen, and the real world which is brutal, lonely and unfair.

EXAMINER'S TIP: WRITING ABOUT WARNINGS

There are warnings throughout the novel about what will happen at the end. We know what happens when Lennie strokes anything – he does not know and cannot control his own strength, and so he kills the things he strokes. The death of the puppy warns us what will happen if Lennie touches Curley's wife, and we already know what happened when he touched a girl's dress in Weed.

Yet despite all this, Steinbeck still makes Lennie seem very innocent. He simply likes to touch soft things, like a child. Tragically for him, he has the mind of a child but the body of a very strong man.

KEY QUOTE

'Lennie never done it in meanness ... All the time he done bad things, but he never done one of 'em mean.' (p. 104)

Section Six: The end of the dream

SUMMARY

1. Lennie waits for George in the clearing by the pool – 'Hide in the brush an' wait for George', he says to himself.

2. He sees a vision of his Aunt Clara, who reprimands him.

3. A vision of a giant rabbit tells Lennie that George will leave him.

4. George arrives and comforts Lennie, and then shoots him dead – 'I want you to stay with me here.'

5. Slim comforts George and tells him he had no choice.

KEY QUOTE

'You hadda, George. I swear, you hadda.' (p. 117)

CHECKPOINT 4

Is it fair to say that the ending seems artificial, too obviously designed for effect rather than being true to life?

WHY IS THIS SECTION IMPORTANT?

A It brings the novel to a **dramatic climax**.
B It **finishes** the novel **back where it started**.
C It introduces for the first and last time **two fantasy visions**.
D At the same time, it shows us **Steinbeck's brilliance** at **natural description**.
E It shows us the tragic but perhaps **inevitable ending** to **George and Lennie's relationship**.

THE SETTING: BACKGROUND TO DEATH

The section opens with a description reminiscent of the opening of the novel. In that opening, there was a heron and a water snake. Now the heron kills the water snake, preparing us for the death of Lennie.

Note the marvellous image of the sun blazing on the Gabilan mountains, and the contrast with the shade of the pool. Here, as before, Steinbeck makes use of light in his descriptions. In addition, 'tiny wind waves' on the water remind us of the waves caused by Lennie in the opening section.

THE VISIONS

DID YOU KNOW

Mechanisation (the introduction of machinery) was about to destroy ranch life as shown by Steinbeck, and the jobs of people such as Slim.

The visions – of Aunt Clara and the giant rabbit – are poetic, and very different from Steinbeck's style in the rest of the novel.

They have been condemned as being unrealistic and totally beyond the ability of a limited mind such as Lennie's to generate. The giant rabbit in particular might appear ridiculous rather than poetic.

However, both visions provide a clear insight into Lennie's feelings at the close of the novel. They show both his guilt and his genuine inability to control himself – a giant with the mind of a baby. They also show how much Lennie suffers – both Aunt Clara and the rabbit hurt Lennie deeply by challenging him on how he rewards George for his care.

KEY QUOTE

'I tried, Aunt Clara, ma'am. I tried and tried.' (p. 111)

GRADE BOOSTER

Slim says of the murder, 'You hadda, George'. Do you agree? What would have been the alternative?

EXAMINER'S TIP: WRITING ABOUT IRONY

There is a tremendous irony in the fact that George takes Carlson's pistol in case he has to kill Lennie as an act of mercy. His decision to kill Lennie in order to protect him is based on the paradox of being cruel to be kind.

DRAMATIC TENSION

There is significant dramatic tension in the last scene. We know that George is going to kill Lennie, but the reader has to wait while the two go over old ground, almost as if George is running over for the last time ever the words he has exchanged so often with Lennie.

There is clear dramatic irony in the comparison between the opening and closing scenes of the novel – the same setting, once filled with hope, is now a scene of despair.

Progress and revision check

REVISION ACTIVITY

1. What happened at Weed that caused Lennie and George to leave? (Write your answers below)

....

2. What happens to Candy's dog?

....

3. What happens when Curley picks a fight with Lennie?

....

4. Why is Lennie in the barn when Curley's wife comes in?

....

5. Where does Lennie go to be alone after killing Curley's wife?

....

REVISION ACTIVITY

On a piece of paper write down answers to these questions:

● What earlier events in the story **foreshadow** the way Lennie kills Curley's wife?

Start: *We know that Lennie and George had to leave Weed because ...*

● In what way could it be said that the story comes full circle (returning to where it began)?

Start: *The novel opens with Lennie and George arriving at a ...*

GRADE BOOSTER

Answer this longer, practice question about the plot/action of the novel:

Q: In what ways could it be said that the novel is highly structured? Think about ...

● The way events or actions are repeated or mirrored.

● The way events slowly build up to a climax.

For a C grade: convey your ideas clearly and appropriately (you could use the words from the question to guide your answer) and refer to details from the text (use specific examples).

For an A grade: make sure you comment on the varied ways the story is structured, perhaps also exploring the effect of the different settings on the structure, and if possible come up with your own original or alternative ideas.

Slim

WHO IS SLIM?

Slim is a 'jerkline skinner', in control of a team of horses, and is seen as the leading worker in the bunk house.

WHAT DOES SLIM DO IN THE NOVEL?

Slim meets George and Lennie in the bunk house (see pp. 36–8).

Slim gives a puppy to Lennie (see pp. 40, 46–7).

Slim agrees that Candy's dog must be killed (see pp. 49–50).

Slim makes Curley promise not to blame Lennie for hurting his hand (see pp. 70–1).

Slim is the one who checks Curley's wife to confirm she is dead (see pp. 105).

Slim comforts George for having killed Lennie (see pp. 117–18).

HOW IS SLIM DESCRIBED AND WHAT DOES IT MEAN?

Quotation	Means?
He is 'godlike' and 'moved with majesty'	Suggests an attractive, almost-princely appearance, confirmed by Curley's suspicions (that Slim is attractive to his wife) and how the men admire and look up to him.
'understanding beyond thought'	He doesn't need to think things through to 'get them'; he realises instinctively how George and Lennie get along, what Lennie is like, and why George had to kill Lennie.
'there was gravity in his manner … all talk stopped when he spoke'	He is respected and listened to; and what he has to say usually has 'gravity' – power and importance.
'His hands, large and lean, were as delicate in their action as those of a temple dancer'	His hands are masculine and strong, but also seem skilful and tender, implying he is almost like an artist, or performer, as the **simile** suggests.

EXAMINER'S TIP: WRITING ABOUT SLIM

When you are writing about Slim make sure you focus on the right thing. Is it what he does, or what he seems to represent or **symbolise** (decency, the conscience of the novel) that is important or both? Whatever you say about him, make sure you get across not only the idea of his general decency, but also his practical understanding – he knows that life is hard, and that dreams don't come true. He drowns some of the puppies because the mother 'couldn't feed that many'. But despite being charismatic, prince-like, understanding and skilled at what he does, Steinbeck also implies that Slim is trapped by the life he leads.

GRADE BOOSTER

To boost your own ideas, find two more quotations about Slim. Draw your own table and write in the second column what you think each quotation means.

EXAMINER'S TIP

Physical descriptions are only worth mentioning in written responses if they add to our understanding of character or behaviour. Slim's hands are worth mentioning for this reason.

CHECKPOINT 5

Is Slim a cruel man?

George

GRADE BOOSTER

Draw up a list of what other characters in the novel say about George. Opposite each quotation, write down exactly what we learn about George from the quotation.

WHO IS GEORGE?

George Milton is an itinerant farm worker, one of many who travel round the country from job to job with no permanent base or home. He is Lennie's friend and companion.

WHAT DOES GEORGE DO IN THE NOVEL?

- He promises Lennie's Aunt Clara that he will look after Lennie (see pp. 43–4).

- After originally mistreating Lennie he cares for him, despite considerable inconvenience and even risk (see p. 44).

- He finds work for himself and Lennie (see p. 6).

- He rescues and protects Lennie when Lennie gets into trouble. We hear about what happened in Weed. The implication is that this is not the first time (see pp. 45–6).

- He feeds Lennie the dream of them both owning a small ranch (see pp. 14–16).

- He orders Lennie to fight back against Curley (see p. 69).

- He leaves Lennie to go to the local brothel with the other ranch hands, showing the part of him that wants to be free from Lennie (see p. 75).

- He shoots Lennie dead, knowing this is kinder to Lennie than being lynched or locked up (see p. 116).

HOW IS GEORGE DESCRIBED AND WHAT DOES IT MEAN?

EXAMINER'S TIP

You will know a lot about George when you've studied the novel. It is always tempting to put down everything you know in a written answer. But you only get marks for points that answer what the examiner asks. For example, if the question asks if George is justified in shooting Lennie, the fact that George lives cleanly is not relevant.

Quotation	Means?
George is 'small and quick, dark of face, with restless eyes and sharp, strong features'.	This suggests intelligence, a strong personality but also some unhappiness ('restless eyes').
'What the hell kind of bed you giving us, anyways. We don't want no pants rabbits.'	George is clean-living and healthy.
'I ain't nothing to scream about, but [Lennie] there can put up more grain alone than most pairs can.'	George is modest.
'"I ain't got no people," George said, "I seen the guys that go around the ranches on their own. That ain't no good. They don't have no fun. After a long time they get mean."'	George is caring, but also frightened of being lonely.
'You keep away from Curley, Lennie.'	George is a good judge of character, and can sense danger.

Quotation	Means?
'Get 'im, Lennie.'	He has a sense of justice, and will not allow Lennie to be beaten up.
Slim: 'That ain't no good, George.' George: 'I know, I know.'	Slim means Lennie could not survive being locked up. In killing a man he loves, George is heroic.

EXAMINER'S TIP: WRITING ABOUT GEORGE

- George symbolises the itinerant farm worker – basically decent men trapped by their jobs and haunted by loneliness. These men have little or no control over their lives. George's dream of owning a tiny patch of land and becoming independent makes his life bearable. It is also the dream of thousands of other similar workers – as Crooks says, 'Ever' body wants a little piece of lan''. When Lennie dies, so does the dream.

- When writing about George be careful not to over-simplify what he is and what he does. It would be easy to see him as a hero who cares for Lennie as a father might. Make sure you note what it costs George to do what he does – 'If I was alone I could live so easy'. In joining the other ranch hands for a night on the town, George shows that part of him yearns for a 'normal' life.

- One of the points made in the novel through George is that intelligence on its own is worth little. If it were worth much, then both George and Crooks would be rich men, because both are obviously intelligent.

- George's companionship with Lennie staves off loneliness, but it also gives him a role in life. He has a clear task, looking after Lennie. Early on it made George feel superior. Now it simply makes him different, and even gives him status. In addition, just as there is trouble in being with Lennie, so there is strength; as George says to Slim: 'We kinda look after each other.' Who would fight George if they knew they would have to fight Lennie as well?

- Does George show 'moral growth' over the course of the novel? His relationship with Lennie matures him, forces him to think more and increases his awareness of moral problems. Early on he used to show off the power he had over Lennie – 'Made me seem God damn smart alongside of him' – forcing him to do stupid and, in one instance, life-threatening things. His sense of shame soon stopped him. However, his shooting of Lennie is the result of everything we have learnt about him and is almost inevitable. Features which George has possessed all along combine to force him to shoot Lennie.

- George is full of compassion and it is this which makes him wish for a clean death for Lennie, rather than a lynching or a lifetime spent cooped up in jail.

- Why does George shoot Lennie? George is a responsible person. He brought Lennie to the farm, and so the responsibility for what happened and for the punishment are his. He accepts them, with great heroism. Slim spots that George had to do what he does to Lennie: 'You hadda, George. I swear you hadda.'

KEY CONNECTIONS

Gary Sinise, who played George in the 1992 version, is a real Steinbeck fan. As a young man his favourite book was *Of Mice and Men*, and he has also starred in a stage production of *The Grapes of Wrath*. Sinise directed the 1992 film too!

CHECKPOINT 6

How is George's physical cleanliness emphasised in the novel?

Lennie

WHO IS LENNIE?

Lennie Small, an itinerant farm worker like George, has a child's mind in a man's body, and as Slim observes, 'He's jes' like a kid' (p. 47). But, as George replies, while Lennie's mind is extremely childlike, 'he's so strong' (p. 47). He is a simpleton, and his tragedy is that his mind has never learnt how to control his body.

CHECKPOINT 7

Note the way that throughout the text Lennie is associated with animals. Would it be better if he was associated more with children?

WHAT DOES LENNIE DO IN THE NOVEL?

- Lennie appears with George, his travelling companion, by a pool in the Salinas River (see p. 2).

- Lennie tries to hide a dead mouse from George (see pp. 5–10).

- Lennie makes George tell the familiar story of the small farm he means to buy (see pp. 14–16).

- Lennie signs up for work at the ranch (see pp. 23–5).

- Lennie is picked on by Curley, the Boss's son (see pp. 27–8).

- Lennie admires Curley's wife – 'Gosh, she was purty' (see p. 35).

- He meets Slim in the bunk house (see pp. 36–8), and Slim gives Lennie a puppy.

- Curley comes to the bunk house and picks a fight with Lennie, who eventually crushes Curley's hand when ordered to retaliate by George (see pp. 68–71).

- Lennie talks to Crooks, and gets angry with him when Crooks suggests George will leave him (see pp. 74–80).

- Lennie kills the puppy Slim has given him and tries to bury it in the barn (see pp. 92–3).

- Curley's wife enters the barn and encourages Lennie to stroke her hair. When she feels Lennie's strength she panics, and Lennie shakes her to death (see pp. 94–100).

- Lennie hides by the pool where we first saw him, and is shot by George (see pp. 109–17).

EXAMINER'S TIP

Remember that Lennie has one of the most distinctive ways of speaking of all the characters in the novel. In writing about him look at how much of what we know about Lennie is based on what comes out of his own mouth.

HOW IS LENNIE DESCRIBED AND WHAT DOES IT MEAN?

Quotation	Means?
He is 'a huge man, shapeless of face … and he walked … the way a bear drags his paws. His arms … hung loosely.'	Suggests Lennie's size and strength, but also that he is simple and animal-like.
'An' I won't get no mice stole from me.'	Lennie may be childlike and innocent, but he knows how to make George feel guilty.

Quotation	Means?
'Come on George. Tell me. Please, George. Like you done before.'	Lennie delights in his and George's dream of a small farm, like a child with a favourite, familiar story.
[Lennie] can put up more grain alone than most pairs can.'	Lennie is incredibly strong and George sees it as an asset in their work.
'He was so scairt he couldn't let go of that dress. And he's so damn strong, you know.'	Tells us that Lennie hangs on and uses his strength when he is scared.
'Sure he's jes' like a kid. There ain't no more harm in him than a kid neither, except he's so strong.'	Emphasises Lennie's childlike simplicity and his strength.
'I didn't want no trouble.'	Lennie doesn't mean to do harm. He just doesn't realise his own strength.
'Me an' him goes ever' place together.'	Lennie is totally dependent on George.
'Why do you got to get killed? You ain't so little as mice. I didn't bounce you hard.'	Lennie blames the animals he kills for their own death, because they are 'tiny', unwilling to blame himself.
'I done a real bad thing,' he said, 'I shouldn't have did that. George'll be mad.'	Lennie reveals that he cannot control himself, and he has no moral judgement. Things are 'good' or 'bad' to Lennie depending on what George will think of them.

GRADE BOOSTER

Write down all the times we are told of Lennie 'petting' something so that it dies, and hanging on violently to something when he is scared. Add to this list all the times when we are warned that Curley and Curley's wife threaten 'trouble' for Lennie. Do all these mean that the ending of the novel simply confirms the inevitable?

DID YOU KNOW

Steinbeck based Lennie on a real person he had known, who was sent to a lunatic asylum for stabbing a ranch boss in the stomach with a pitchfork.

EXAMINER'S TIP: WRITING ABOUT LENNIE

A C grade description of Lennie will show his huge strength, his innocence and his childlike simplicity. He is amazed and upset when his mice and his puppy die, unable to realise that it is not their fragility but his strength that are to blame. Lennie is 'a nice fella'.

For an A grade, you might point out that Steinbeck's portrayal is more complex than this. He describes Lennie in terms of an animal more than a child. Animals are innocent, in that they do not have the capacity to act morally or know good from bad. But animals can be dangerous because they can have no morals and act on instinct. Steinbeck compares Lennie to a bear, a potentially very dangerous animal. Lennie drags his feet 'the way a bear drags his paws'. The only way he can cope is to be a like a tame dog, tethered always to his master George and never let out of his master's sight. Yet Lennie can also be like a wild dog, needing to be 'put down' by his owner.

Candy

WHO IS CANDY?

Candy has lost his right hand in a farm accident and is now reduced to the meanest job on the ranch – that of 'swamper' or menial cleaner.

WHAT DOES CANDY DO IN THE NOVEL?

- Candy introduces George and Lennie to the bunk house and to the Boss (see pp. 19–23).
- He warns George and Lennie against Curley (see pp. 28–9).
- Candy allows the ranch hand Carlson to shoot his old, smelly dog (see pp. 51–3).
- Candy offers his $300 savings to help buy George and Lennie's farm, if he can join them (see p. 65)
- Candy joins Crooks and Lennie in the harness room, Crooks's home, and briefly tries to stand up to Curley's wife (see pp. 82–5).
- Candy discovers the dead body of Curley's wife in the barn (see pp. 101–2).

HOW IS CANDY DESCRIBED AND WHAT DOES IT MEAN?

Quotation	Means?
Candy is a 'Tall, stoop shouldered old man', who has lost his right hand.	Right from the start Candy's age and his physical weakness are emphasised.
Candy is also described through his dog, 'a drag-footed sheep dog, grey of muzzle and with pale, blind old eyes'.	Candy's relationship with his dog is like George's relationship with Lennie, not something rational but an antidote to loneliness. Candy, rather like his dog, is old, infirm and weak. One of the strongest statements in *Of Mice and Men* is that such people are worthy of our attention and our respect.

EXAMINER'S TIP: WRITING ABOUT CANDY

Think about just how little it would take to revitalise Candy – ten acres and a few animals. We see Candy (along with Lennie) 'grinning with delight' when he plans the ranch with George and Lennie. Steinbeck is perhaps asking us not to judge by appearances, and see people for who they are inside.

GRADE BOOSTER

We are shown Candy as an old, disabled man, a 'no-body'. Was he always like this, or has he been ground down by the life he has had to lead. Write down any hints in the novel that Candy was once a more powerful, effective person. As one of your points, mention the brief moment he stands up to Curley's wife.

EXAMINER'S TIP

It's an old saying that dogs take after their owners. When writing about Candy, remember how much of our image of him comes from the description, and the fate, of his dog.

Curley

WHO IS CURLEY?

urley is the Boss's son, a small, aggressive young man with a rudge against the world and a reputation as a fighter.

WHAT DOES CURLEY DO IN THE NOVEL?

Curley comes in to the bunk house when George and Lennie arrive and is aggressive towards them, for no reason (see pp. 27–8).

He bursts into the bunk house looking for his wife, thinking she is with Slim (see pp. 58–9).

He picks a fight with Lennie but has his hand crushed when Lennie is told to fight back by George (see pp. 68–70).

At Slim's urging he agrees to say the injury was the result of an accident with a farm machine (see pp. 70–1).

Curley leads the mob hunting for Lennie after the killing of Curley's wife, announcing that he wants to shoot Lennie 'in the guts' (see p. 106).

HOW IS CURLEY DESCRIBED AND WHAT DOES IT MEAN?

Quotation	Means?
He hates big guys. He's alla time picking scraps with big guys. Kind of like he's mad at 'em because he ain't a big guy.'	Curley seems set on proving that he is a big man in all but size. His success as an amateur boxer is an obsession, so every person he meets is seen as a possible opponent.
Curley says he's keeping that hand oft for his wife.'	Curley makes obscene allusions to his wife and goes to the brothel on Saturday nights.
I don't *like* Curley. He ain't a nice fella.'	Curley only sees the world through his eyes and so is supremely selfish. His inability to control or understand his wife brings about Lennie's death. He is to blame, just as much as his wife or Lennie, but will never accept that.

EXAMINER'S TIP: WRITING ABOUT CURLEY

There is a lot to write about Curley, but something that is often missed is the comment by Candy at the start of the novel, that Curley 'won't ever get canned [sacked or dismissed] 'cause his old man's the boss'. Curley's power is huge and a good example of social injustice and corruption. Injustice is a **theme** and is presented as a fact of life in *Of Mice and Men*. Curley is a major figure in revealing the injustice of the world the ranch hands live and work in.

GRADE BOOSTER

Why is Curley so hostile to big men? One character in the novel attempts an explanation. Find it, and then try to say the same thing in your own words. Ask yourself why Curley agrees not to blame Lennie for his 'busted' hand. Is it because he does not want to offend Slim? Or because if he admits to what happened he will be laughed at?

EXAMINER'S TIP

Curley is the most unpleasant character in the novel. Be careful when writing about him not just to list all the bad things about him, but try also to say why he might be as he is.

Curley's wife

WHO IS CURLEY'S WIFE?

She is the young, attractive newly married wife of Curley, the Boss's son.

WHAT DOES SHE DO IN THE NOVEL?

- She makes Curley jealous by flirting with the ranch hands.
- She creates tension in the bunk house.
- She is killed by Lennie, and is therefore the reason that George has to shoot him.

HOW IS SHE DESCRIBED AND WHAT DOES IT MEAN?

Quotation	Means?
'She had full, rouged lips and wide-spaced eyes, heavily made up. Her fingernails were red. Her hair hung in little rolled clusters, like sausages.'	Curley's wife is described as a 'tart' and is seen as 'jail bait' by the ranch hands.
'Think I'm gonna stay in that two-by-four house and listen how Curley's gonna lead with his left twice, and then bring in the ol' right cross?'	Curley's wife is very lonely, as are so many people in the novel, and is trapped in a loveless marriage.
'You know what I can do to you if you open your trap?'	She can be vindictive and she will use the power her status gives her, even if it is totally unfair.
'He says he was gonna put me in the movies.'	Curley's wife has her dream destroyed too.
'She was very pretty and simple, and her face was sweet and young.'	Curley's wife is never really evil. Her punishment outweighs any crimes she may have committed.

EXAMINER'S TIP: WRITING ABOUT CURLEY'S WIFE

We know more about Steinbeck's feelings towards Curley's wife than about any other character. In the famous 'Miss Luce' letter, he wrote to the actress playing the part in the stage version of the novel and explained how he saw the character. In the letter, Steinbeck says she is essentially a good and trusting person who grew up 'in an atmosphere of fighting and suspicion'. Her pretence of hardness is largely a sham. It is all she knows. She is not particularly over-sexed, but has been forced to recognise that her sexuality is the only weapon she has, and the only thing that gets her noticed.

GRADE BOOSTER

Steinbeck never provides a name for Curley's wife. Think how this affects our response to her. Start off with 'The fact that Curley's wife is never named helps create the impression of her as someone with no individual existence of her own …'.

EXAMINER'S TIP

Use the internet or a library to access the 'Miss Luce letter' that Steinbeck wrote to the actress playing Curley's wife. We know from this letter what Steinbeck wanted to achieve in his portrayal. Summarise all his points, and write down opposite each one if you think he actually achieved them.

Crooks

WHO IS CROOKS?

rooks is the 'stable buck' for the ranch, the man who provides
e support for the many horses and mules the farm uses. He has
bent or 'busted' spine and the characters refer to him by a
rm we find very offensive today.

WHAT DOES CROOKS DO IN THE NOVEL?

Crooks tells Slim that Lennie is handling the pups (see p. 55).

Crooks lets Lennie talk to him in Crooks' own room on the
Saturday night when all the other hands are at Susy's brothel (see pp. 75–91).

Crooks taunts Lennie with the idea that George might desert him, and is
frightened by Lennie's response (see pp. 78–80).

Candy and then Curley's wife joins them, and when Crooks challenges her and
demands that she leave, she humiliates him with the threat that she will accuse
him of rape (pp. 88–9).

Having initially been drawn in to George and Lennie's dream of a small farm,
Crooks withdraws his support (see p. 91).

HOW IS CROOKS DESCRIBED AND WHAT DOES IT MEAN?

Quotation	Means?
Nice fella too. Got a crooked back where a horse kicked him. The boss gives him hell when he's mad. But the stable buck don't give a damn about that. He reads a lot. Got books in his room.'	Despite being the 'stable buck', Crooks is proud, independent and intelligent. But none of these admirable features stop the boss from giving him 'hell'.
Crooks was a proud, aloof man … his eyes .. seemed to glitter with intensity … he had thin, pain tightened lips.'	Crooks's life is dominated by pain – the pain of being the only black man and of his 'busted back' – but he has managed to rise above that pain.
I ain't wanted in the bunk house … 'Cause 'm black.'	Crooks is a victim of racial prejudice.
'"I had enough," he said coldly. "You got no rights comin' in a colored man's room."'	Crooks has enough pride and independence to stand up to Curley's wife.
'Crooks had reduced himself to nothing. There was no personality, no ego – nothing to arouse either like or dislike.'	The futility of Crooks's stand shows how little real power a black person has in the world of this novel.

CHECKPOINT 8

What items does
Crooks own?

★ **GRADE BOOSTER**

Crooks is
sarcastic and
uses **irony**. We
sympathise with
him because he
suffers racial
discrimination
and is disabled,
but try thinking
about the ways
he does not help
himself and
perhaps
contributes to
his own
loneliness. One
example might
be his pulling
out of the deal
he seems willing
to make with
George, Lennie
and Candy to
work on their
farm.

CROOKS continued

Quotation	Means?
'Nobody gets to heaven, and nobody gets no land.'	Crooks has a double burden. He is not only a black man in a society that immediately discriminates against non-whites, but is also partly disabled in a society that values human beings on their ability to provide a service.
'You guys is just kiddin' yourself. You'll talk about it a hell of a lot, but you won't get no land.'	Crooks's structural role in the novel is to appear two-thirds of the way in and to **forewarn** and prepare you for the destruction of George and Lennie's dream.

GRADE BOOSTER

Look at the way Crooks seems almost to delight in taunting Lennie that George will leave him, until he is frightened by Lennie's response. Is Crooks one of those people who take comfort in making other people as unhappy as he is?

EXAMINER'S TIP: WRITING ABOUT CROOKS

When writing about Crooks, it is easy to see him in the perspective of the modern world, where we are much more sensitive about issues of race and disability. Remember the times. In Steinbeck's time many types of people who are now protected by law – black people, the disabled, women, old people – had no such protection. Write about Crooks as Steinbeck writes about him: a man who through no fault of his own has been sidelined as unimportant. Steinbeck's aim is to tell us that the people society says are unimportant really do matter.

In creating Crooks, Steinbeck is following a tradition, which you can join in with. First, find a character in whom you have to believe, because he or she is so convincingly drawn and you identify with them. Then expose him or her to a potent dream and show him or her warming to it as you have warmed to it. Finally, show the character realising that the dream is nothing more than a dream, a fantasy doomed to failure because the real world does not allow dreams to come to fruition. Like Crooks, we want to believe in the dream despite everything we know. And like Crooks, we come to realise that it is an impossible dream.

Minor characters

- **The Boss** is a stocky, short little man. He is a reasonable sort of person, who gets angry at times but buys whisky for the hands at Christmas. He is a very distant figure. His wife is never mentioned and it might be assumed that she is dead.

- **Carlson** is 'a powerful, big-stomached man' who is an insensitive ranch hand. He objects to the smell of Candy's dog and pressurises Candy to have it shot. He commits the act himself with evident satisfaction, using his own Luger pistol. This is the same pistol that George later uses to shoot Lennie.

- **Whit** is a young ranch hand, who finds a letter in a magazine written by an ex-worker at the ranch. He is very superficial, and has no real involvement in the plot of the novel or its **themes**, except as the hand who is sent into the town to fetch the deputy sheriff after the murder of Curley's wife.

Progress and revision check

REVISION ACTIVITY

❶ How long has Curley been married to his wife? (Write your answers below)

....

❷ What injury has Candy suffered?

....

❸ What injury has Crooks suffered?

....

❹ Who brought up Lennie and handed him over to George to care for?

....

❺ Who owns the Luger pistol George uses to kill Lennie?

....

REVISION ACTIVITY

On a piece of paper write down answers to these questions:

● Which of the characters appear to you as victims, and which appear to have control over their lives?

● How many of those characters can be said to be lonely?

● How common is it for Steinbeck to give each character a simple, short physical introductory description?

GRADE BOOSTER

Answer this longer, practice question about the characters of the novel:

Q: Does Steinbeck simply admire those characters with physical skills? Think about …

● The praise he heaps on Slim.

● The fact that many of the lesser characters are clearly intelligent.

For a C grade: show how the physical skills of Slim do allow Steinbeck to praise him, and how Lennie gains praise for his physical strength. Use quotations to support your answer.

For an A grade: shows how Steinbeck clearly admires the 'clever' people in the novel, such as George and Crooks. Explore also how intelligence gives characters in the novel no real control over their lives.

Key contexts

THE AUTHOR

A key figure in Steinbeck's success was his father. He supported his son through the bleak years when he was trying to establish himself. Outwardly there was little to justify his belief in his son. Steinbeck's first novel, *Cup of Gold*, was rejected several times before finding a publisher in 1929, and even then it failed financially.

Steinbeck's literary agents, McIntosh and Otis, were also crucial to his success. They took him on in 1931 and kept faith in him when no one else seemed to believe he had a future as a writer. In 1962, when he was awarded the Nobel Prize for Literature, he insisted that McIntosh and Otis take a percentage of the very considerable prize money.

Steinbeck was a lonely, modest and restless man. He was never content and always searched for something more. He was difficult to live with, yet easy to love, something he shares with many great writers and artists. His love of the outdoors, of animals and of individual human beings shines through in *Of Mice and Men*.

THE AMERICAN DREAM

Poor and oppressed people the world over were attracted to America from the time of its discovery. Conditions were hard for the early settlers, but 'The American Dream' was of freedom, independence and owning one's own land. The dream was a real possibility while there was still a 'frontier' of unclaimed land, but by 1900 there was no unsettled land in America, and in reality the dream was over. It still survived in the popular imagination and in literature at least until the late 1920s. By then America had built its own aristocracy on the basis of wealth and its own system of repression based on race. The final blow was dealt by the Wall Street Crash, when the value of shares on the stock market fell dramatically. This marked the start of the Great Depression that swept the world in the 1930s. Farming was as badly affected as any other area of the economy. Decay there was sped up because ignorance and over-farming had resulted in hundreds of thousands of acres of farmland drying up, losing precious top soil and being turned into the famous 'dust bowl'. Poor crops meant that many farmers were unable to repay the debts they had taken out to buy their land.

Thus the way of life for men such as George, Lennie and Slim was coming to an end when *Of Mice and Men* was written, pushed by the twin forces of mechanisation and economic recession. George and Lennie's dream of freedom and independence was probably over before they acquired it. Lennie makes George recite their dream to him at the end of the novel, not realising that George is preparing to shoot him before he is lynched by the pursuing mob. Lennie dies at George's hands in an act of mercy. The dream they and many other migrant workers shared – 'We gonna get a little place' – is as doomed as Lennie.

KEY CONNECTIONS

Get a copy of the text for the play *Of Mice and Men* from a library and compare it with the novel. What has been left out from the novel and what has been added in? What does this tell you about the different style required for plays and novels?

 **DID YOU KNOW**

In his acceptance speech for the Nobel Prize in 1962, Steinbeck said that a writer should expose human 'faults and failures', but that any worthy author will 'passionately believe in the perfectibility of man'.

Of Mice and Men

Sometimes a novel will hint at its **theme** through its title. The title of *Of Mice and Men* appears to be taken from the poem 'To a Mouse' by the Scottish poet Robert Burns (1759–96): 'The best laid schemes o' mice and men / Gang aft agley / And leave us nought but grief and pain / For promised joy!'

It is not difficult to see the link with Steinbeck's novel: 'Gang aft agley' means 'often go wrong'. George and Lennie's best-laid scheme for a small farm does go wrong, and leaves grief and pain where there should have been joy. Burns's poem also suggests that grief and pain, instead of joy, affect all creatures in nature, not just humanity.

At the heart of the poem is the feeling that we are free to make our plans and lay our schemes, but we are far less free or likely to achieve them. Steinbeck never suggests that the likelihood of grief and pain should be a reason to stop humans trying their plans. We need to have these plans or dreams in order to survive, for all that they might hurt us.

Setting and Place

The setting of *Of Mice and Men* is clearly identified as a real setting – the Salinas River 'a few miles south of Soledad'. It is vividly, almost lovingly, described. Most of the action takes place on the ranch, and it unusual for the action of a novel to happen in such a limited space. The setting helps give the idea that George and Lennie are simply a passing part of nature, like the heron, the water snake and the leaves Steinbeck describes. The single place in which the action happens gives the novel a concentrated sense of identity, and at times makes it dramatic, as if this was a play that we were watching.

Examiner's tip: Writing about setting and culture

When you write about the setting of the novel, remember that when Steinbeck wrote *Of Mice and Men* he was not simply writing a guide to nature. What he was writing was a book about human dreams, loneliness and people who cannot control or escape from their lives. The setting is only important where it throws light on the themes and **characters** of the novel, as when the description of the heron killing the water snake or Lennie drinking 'scummy' water prepare us for events that come later.

Remember that the novel is set in a different culture, one in which there are still wide open spaces, such as the pool, uninhabited by man. It is also a culture in which men's physical skills – lifting grain or controlling a line of mules or horses – command respect, rather than simply showing their control over machinery.

> **CHECKPOINT 9**
>
> Do you think Steinbeck is too gloomy and pessimistic in describing the world of the ranch hands?

Key themes

HUMAN FRAGILITY

The overriding **theme** of the novel is that humanity is small and fragile in comparison with the forces that control our lives. Joy is something to be snatched while possible, but is not something that most humans ever achieve for long. There is no real thematic link between the mice in the title and the mice that Lennie likes to stroke. Lennie's mice are used rather as a **motif** that echoes his vulnerability throughout the novel.

REVISION ACTIVITY

Look at the following passages that highlight the theme of human fragility: where Lennie is talking about how easily the mice he pets die (p. 10); the section on the shooting of Candy's dog (pp. 48–52); Curley's wife's corpse (p. 101); the death of Lennie (pp. 115–16). What strikes you most about these examples?

DREAMS AND REALITY

One of Steinbeck's themes in *Of Mice and Men* is the dreams that people have. George and Lennie's dream is of a very small farm, a patch of land which they own themselves. It is a dream of working for themselves, of being independent, and it is a dream sufficiently powerful to draw in Candy and, temporarily, even the cynical Crooks. We also know it is a dream shared by many thousands of itinerant ranch hands.

Yet this is not the only dream in the novel. Curley's wife has a pathetic dream of being a movie star; and the ranch hands dream of being the cowboy heroes they read about in the pulp magazines.

REVISION ACTIVITY

Look at the following passages that highlight this theme: the first telling of George and Lennie's dream (pp. 14–16); the dream of the ranch hands that they are romantic cowboys (pp. 50–1); the second telling of George and Lennie's dream to Candy (pp. 61–4); the dream of Curley's wife to be a movie star (pp. 96–7).

Write down a list of all the times we are told or hinted at that George and Lennie's dream will never come true. Write down all the other dreams people have in the novel, and decide whether any of those have a chance of coming true.

What is the impact on the reader of these failed hopes and personal dreams? Does it allow us to empathise or feel pity for the main characters, or despise them?

DID YOU KNOW

Steinbeck once said, 'Ideas are like rabbits. You get a couple and learn how to handle them, and pretty soon you have a dozen.'

KEY CONNECTIONS

A 1981 version for television was made as the result of a lifelong ambition on the part of producer/star Robert Blake. It is hard to get hold of, but is seen as an above average production.

EXAMINER'S TIP: WRITING ABOUT DREAMS

If you are writing about dreams, remember there is more than one dream in the novel, as well as George and Lennie's dream of a small farm. There is the wider American Dream of freedom and independence, the dream Curley's wife has as a movie star and perhaps even Curley's dream of being a champion boxer.

For higher grades, consider your personal response: do these sorts of dreams seem relevant today? Or are they specific to Steinbeck's time and culture?

PESSIMISM OR OPTIMISM?

Is *Of Mice and Men* a pessimistic book? Its ending is unhappy, yet much in it is optimistic. George's care for Lennie, Lennie's adoration of George and the natural dignity of Slim are all positive, good things. Nor is Lennie's death wholly pessimistic. Lennie dies at the hand of the one man he trusts, painlessly, happy, free, in the open and still believing in his dream – as perhaps he might have died on the farm had they ever bought it. Lennie's death can be seen as an act of kindness, not of vengeance. Alternatively you could even compare it to the killing of the water snake by the heron at the end of the book and see both as part of life and nature: so inevitable that human comment on them is almost superfluous.

REVISION ACTIVITY

Look at the introductory description of Slim (pp. 36–7) and the killing of Lennie (pp. 115–17). How do they compare?

PROTEST AND RACIAL PREJUDICE

Another frequently asked question is the extent to which *Of Mice and Men* is a political novel, or a novel of protest. The ranch hands get their fifty dollars a month plus food and shelter, seem to eat well and have a reasonable boss. To that extent the novel is not political. Nor does it concern itself with how the country is governed. If it protests, it does so against three social and political evils: racial discrimination, the treatment of old age and disability, and the plight of the farm worker who never reaps what he sows. Both Candy and Crooks are workers who will never see the benefits of their labour.

Crooks illustrates racial prejudice. He is intelligent, reads books and, like any other human being, he needs warmth and companionship. He is denied these, not through any fault of his own but because he is black. Yet if there is a theme of racial prejudice here it is almost a sub-division of a wider theme, that of loneliness.

REVISION ACTIVITY

Look at the passage where Candy shows he knows what his future holds (p. 66) and where Curley's wife humiliates Crooks (see pp. 88–9). Write down the ways in which they demonstrate this theme.

LONELINESS

Loneliness is a major **theme** in *Of Mice and Men*. George and Lennie stave it off by their relationship. It embitters Candy and Crooks. It kills Curley's wife. Steinbeck sees it as a part of the human condition, something we are born with and something we either fight or succumb to all our lives:

> "Guys like us, that work on ranches, are the loneliest guys in the world" …
> Lennie broke in. "But not us! An' why? Because … because I got you to look
> after me, and you got me to look after you, and that's why."

As with many of the statements in the novel, Steinbeck offers no answers to loneliness, merely a graphic and moving portrayal of the problem. It confirms the impression of him as a writer who observes and brings things to life through the printed word. He is not someone writing with a grand game plan for how to change things. Indeed, some of the sadness and emotional power of the novel comes from our realisation that things cannot and will not change.

KEY CONNECTIONS

For a different perspective on Lennie, see James Whale's film version of *Frankenstein* (1931). The monster finds a small girl throwing flowers into a lake. Thinking that she will float like the flowers, the monster accidentally drowns her. A lynch mob is raised that chases him to his death.

REVISION ACTIVITY

Look at the passages that deal with this theme: the extract quoted above (pp. 14–15); George's confession to Slim, starting 'I ain't got no people' (pp. 45–6); Candy's explanation of his love for his old dog (p. 49); the description of Crooks (pp. 73–4); Curley's wife talking to Lennie, where she says 'I get lonely' (pp. 94–5). Make a list of the different effects of lonliness.

RELATIONSHIPS

You could argue that the theme of relationships is part of the loneliness theme looked at above. Do you think it is an accident that no relationships in *Of Mice and Men* seem able to last for any length of time? The obvious relationship is between George and Lennie, and we see that destroyed. But there is also the relationship between Candy and his dog, the proposed partnership between George, Lennie and Candy and the relationship between Curley and his wife. The happiest people in the novel – Slim, the Boss, Carlson – are the ones who do not seem to be in any kind of relationship. Are relationships simply a guarantee of pain to come, and therefore not worth having?

EXAMINER'S TIP: WRITING ABOUT MICE AND MEN

The title of the book is probably not linked directly to the mice Lennie pets and kills (see **Key contexts**), but it does suggest that mice and men are part of the same system, and that there is little to choose between them in terms of the control they have over their lives. It suggests men are as insignificant as mice. Will Lennie be missed any more than the mice he has killed?

Progress and revision check

REVISION ACTIVITY

1. Look at the passage where Lennie becomes scared of the ranch, senses something bad will happen there and cries out 'Le's go, George. Le's get outta here. It's mean here.' Write down what it tells us about Lennie, then write down other passages or incidents that show how little control he has over things and how things always go wrong for him.

   ....

2. Write down a list of all the times we are told or it is hinted that George and Lennie's dream will never come true. Write down all the other dreams people have in the novel, and decide if any of those have a chance of coming true.

   ....

3. List the reasons for killing Candy's dog, and then list the reasons for George killing Lennie. How similar are they?

   ....

4. Identify and write down every instance in the novel where a character talks about or is shown to be lonely. You might be surprised how important this makes the theme of loneliness look!

   ....

REVISION ACTIVITY

On a piece of paper write down answers to these questions:

- To what extent is *Of Mice and Men* a novel about people's dreams and their inability to make them come true? Remember to look at all the dreams characters have in the novel, and compare the importance of these dreams to other themes in the novel.

- Does the novel suggest that very few people can make relationships that last? Look through all the characters and decide if any of them have had a lasting relationship with anyone else.

GRADE BOOSTER

Q: Do you think that Steinbeck intended *Of Mice and Men* to be an optimistic novel, hopeful about the way things are, or a pessimistic novel and one that always assumes the worst will happen?

For a C grade: explain some of the unhappy things that happen in the novel (what happens to Candy's dog, the death of Curley's wife and Lennie), illustrating how sad they are with quotations and generally providing evidence that the novel is pessimistic.

For an A grade: explore, briefly, all the unhappy events in the novel, but also consider whether there is happiness and goodness in Slim and some of the minor characters, and that many characters are made both happy and optimistic by their dreams. You might conclude that this is a pessimistic novel as far as events go, but also a novel that thinks human beings are valuable and precious. For a high grade, your interpretation and detailed exploration of all aspects of the task are vital.

Language

Here are some useful terms to know when writing about *Of Mice and Men*, what they mean and how they appear in the book.

Literary term	Means?	Example
Irony	Saying one thing but meaning another. **Sarcasm** is a crude form of spoken irony. Authors use irony to show real meanings, meanings which people sometimes hide.	Crooks is being ironic when he says it is 'swell' to have a room with a manure heap outside its window.
Imagery	Images are an author's main means of description. They can be any picture an author summons up, but often consist of either a **simile** (saying one thing is like another) or a **metaphor** (saying one thing is another thing).	Steinbeck uses imagery when he compares Lennie to a bear, saying he walks 'the way a bear drags his paws'. This is a simile. Steinbeck is not saying Lennie is a bear, just that he is like a bear. Imagery is also used when Steinbeck says of Slim that he had a 'hatchet face'. Clearly Slim's face is not a hatchet, but it has some of the features of a hatchet – sharp, hard, clearly defined. By using a metaphor (saying Slim's face is a hatchet) Steinbeck gives more immediacy, drive and force than if he had used a simile, and said Slim's face was 'like' a hatchet.
Dialogue	The way characters speak to each other in a novel or a play.	The **dialogue** in *Of Mice and Men* is very realistic. Steinbeck tried to imitate the way the ranch hands really spoke. He could have had George say 'We have to keep working here until we can gather some money together. We have no option. We'll leave as soon as we can. I do not like this place any more than you do.' As it is, he has George say 'We gotta keep it till we get a stake. We can't help it, Lennie. We'll get out jus' as soon as we can. I don't like it no better than you do.'

CHECKPOINT 10

How much of the novel is written in dialogue, and how much does Steinbeck allow the reader to find out about the **characters** by letting them speak out loud to us?

Literary term	Means?	Example
Theme	A theme is a central idea that an author examines in what he writes.	Themes in *Of Mice and Men* include loneliness; dreams and reality; protest and racial prejudice; optimism and pessimism.
Paradox	Paradox occurs when a statement that appears on the outside to be outrageous is shown to be true.	*Of Mice and Men* is full of paradoxes. Lennie kills Curley's wife and lots of small animals, but is essentially innocent. Curley's wife is a 'tart' and causes her own death and Lennie's, but at the same time is shown to be 'innocent'.

THE TWO STYLES IN *OF MICE AND MEN*

There are two separate styles (ways of writing) in *Of Mice and Men*: descriptive style and dialogue.

Descriptive style

This style is descriptive and almost poetic in its intensity. Steinbeck tends to start a section in this style, often making heavy use of natural description, or a detailed description of the setting in which the action will take place. The description of the harness room in which Crooks lives is a good example. Only once does that style break in unexpectedly rather than coming at the start or the end of a section: when Steinbeck halts the action to deliver what can seem a funeral eulogy (speech) for Curley's wife (see p. 100, starting 'The sun streaks were high on the wall by now').

The style owes its success to Steinbeck's eye for minute observation of nature and his gift for unusual **metaphors** and **similes**. Of course, many of these are not unusual. Lennie is compared twice to a bear, once at the start of the novel and once at the end. This is a simple image. Bears are big, very strong and, in comparison to humans, not very clever, which are obvious links to Lennie.

Some of Steinbeck's **imagery** is more unusual. In one example, he describes the head of a water-snake as being a 'periscope' (p. 109). At first reading this simile might seem totally out of place. A periscope is a man-made object of steel and glass, part of a machine designed for war and found at sea rather than in the confines of a small pool in a river. Yet the image does work because:

- It is startling and unexpected. It focuses your attention on what is being described.

- Visually the water snake and the periscope are similar. Both are upright and ploughing through the water.

- The snake's eyes are in its head, just as the periscope provides eyes for the submarine.

- A submarine is a machine of death, but so perhaps is the snake, hunting for its prey in the shadows.

EXAMINER'S TIP

The examiner will be impressed if you can identify metaphors and talk about the effects they have. Keep a list as you read *Of Mice and Men*.

DID YOU KNOW

The *New York Times* described the novel as 'a thriller, a gripping tale … that you will not set down until it is finished'.

Steinbeck's descriptive style can also be very powerful when he uses straightforward language. For example, George has to stop Lennie from drinking from a pool at the start of the novel. The water is 'scummy' (p. 3). This is a simple, factual description of the water. As well as describing the water, the description manages to tell us how very little common sense Lennie has. Also, by hinting at dirt and corruption, it might even prepare us for a dark ending to the novel.

Steinbeck's style is also very economical. Rather than pouring hundreds of descriptive words into a paragraph, he describes a few bare essentials to give a flavour of the scene.

Use of light: Steinbeck loves to use light in his descriptive passages. The light flaming on the Gabilan Mountains is a recurrent image. Steinbeck is fascinated by sunlight. He describes a bar of it shining into the bunk house:

> the sun threw a bright dust-laden bar through one of the side windows, and in and out of the beam flies shot like rushing stars. **(p. 19)**

Later Curley's wife enters the bunk house and 'the rectangle of sunshine in the doorway was cut off' – the light being used as a **symbol** for the way that her stupidity is going to cut short her own life and Lennie's, and destroy George and Lennie's dream.

Sound and vision: Steinbeck also uses sound in his descriptions, particularly the background sounds that add so much to our imagination of the colour and vision of a scene. One example is 'the thuds and occasional clangs of a horseshoe game' in the yard (p. 42); another is the sounds heard by George as he prepares to kill Lennie:

> the leaves rustled … And the shouts of men sounded again, this time much closer than before. **(p. 114)**

As the men get nearer, the shouts grow louder and the sense of tension is increased. The accuracy of Steinbeck's observation helps you to believe that you are an eyewitness to the events described.

GRADE BOOSTER

Steinbeck's use of light and sound gives a precise sense of perspective and distance in the novel, and fixes the moment clearly in our minds.

EXAMINER'S TIP: WRITING ABOUT STEINBECK'S STYLE

One of the most interesting passages in the novel is on page 101:

> As happens sometimes, a moment settled and hovered and remained for much more than a moment. And sound stopped and movement stopped for much, much more than a moment.

This passage can be described as 'poetic', meaning it is very intense and concentrated. Its real importance is that it is so unusual. It is as if Steinbeck steps out of the shadows where he has been hiding all through the novel and talks directly to the reader. Do you think it works well, emphasising the importance of Curley's wife and her death? Or is it too obvious, with Steinbeck trying too hard to make something seem important that we already know is important?

Dialogue

The second style or way of writing occupies most of the novel. It is down-to-earth, relies on **dialogue** and is **colloquial** (formed from everyday speech). Steinbeck manages to blend these two styles together with almost complete fluency. This blending is one of the reasons why *Of Mice and Men* is such a remarkable novel.

The language of Steinbeck's characters is written down in a way that allows you almost to hear the characters speaking. Steinbeck spells words so as to reflect how they sound in the mouths of ordinary people (this is called 'phonetic spelling'), not how they appear in a dictionary. People leave the beginning and ending off words – Steinbeck writes 'an" for 'and', 'jus" for 'just', 'gonna' for 'going to' – and do not speak 'correct' English, as when Lennie says 'I shouldn't of done that' instead of 'I shouldn't have done that.' Steinbeck uses slang, as when the ranch hands go the local brothel for a 'flop'.

EXAMINER'S TIP: WRITING ABOUT STEINBECK'S LANGUAGE OF SPEECH

Be careful to distinguish between *slang* and *phonetic spelling*. Slang is words or phrases that are in common usage but which may have only a temporary existence. Slang dates quite rapidly. For example, it was very popular in the 1960s to use the word 'fab' (short for 'fabulous'). Using that slang now might seem unusual and out of place. We do not laugh at characters who use slang in *Of Mice and Men* because we recognise that this is how people of that time spoke. Don't confuse slang words and phrases with words and phrases that Steinbeck has spelt to imitate the way people actually said them, as in 'Jes" for 'just'. *Phonetic spelling* (spelling a word or phrase as it sounds) is completely different.

CHECKPOINT 11

Does the use of slang 'date' the novel, fixing it as happening at one time in one area and reducing its universal meaning?

Structure

Of Mice and Men is a short novel. Sometimes short novels are described as 'novellas' The book usually has no chapter divisions, but falls into six readily identifiable sections

A PLAY-LIKE STRUCTURE

The division of the novel into six clear sections bears comparison with the separate scenes of a play, because:

- Each 'scene' has a clearly identified **setting**.
- The setting is **simple** and often very **visual**.
- The **plot** progresses **chronologically**, i.e. in the order in which it actually happens.
- There is a lot of dialogue and speech.
- The characters and the setting are often very **visual**.

There is therefore a **dramatic** element to the structure of the novel as well as to its style.

Why are there no chapter divisions? Probably because in such a short novel Steinbeck does not want to break up the flow of the text. Chapter divisions might also reduce the feeling of inevitability in the novel.

AN INEVITABLE ENDING?

Steinbeck has been criticised for making the ending seem inevitable, and for dropping too many clumsy hints as to what will happen. The hints are:

- Lennie's killing of mice.
- What happened between Lennie and the girl in Weed.
- The killing of Candy's dog.
- The fight with Curley.
- The killing of the puppy.
- The emphasis on Lennie's vast strength.
- Curley's wife's interest in Lennie.
- George's oft-repeated assertions that Curley's wife will bring nothing but trouble

The defence against this charge is that Steinbeck is not writing a novel of suspense, but a novel about characters. However, it might still be felt that some of the hints he offers are rather heavy-handed. Remember that many types of literature do not require you to be kept in suspense.

SIMPLICITY

Of Mice and Men follows a simple chronological, or real time, structure. There are no flashbacks to previous episodes and there is no rushing forward to see snippets of the future, both common techniques in many modern novels. The story commences on a Thursday evening and its climax is reached on the following Sunday afternoon. The keynote of the plot and structure in this novel is simplicity.

DID YOU KNOW

Steinbeck himself dramatised *Of Mice and Men* for the stage.

KEY CONNECTIONS

Steinbeck's *The Grapes of Wrath* has a very similar style to *Of Mice and Men.*

Progress and revision check

REVISION ACTIVITY

1. How many sections is the novel divided in to?

   ....

2. How many of those sections start with a description of the setting?

   ....

3. Count the number of times characters are compared to animals.

   ....

4. Write down all the similarities you can think of between how *Of Mice and Men* is written and how a play is written.

   ....

5. How many times in each section does a character use a slang word or phrase?

   ....

REVISION ACTIVITY

On a piece of paper write down answers to these questions:

● What are the most important features of Steinbeck's language?

   Start: *Steinbeck uses language in two different styles in 'Of Mice and Men' ...*

● Are we made to feel that the ending of the novel is inevitable?

   Start: *Steinbeck gives several hints as to how the novel will end...*

GRADE BOOSTER

Answer this longer, practice question about the themes of the novel:

Q: Is there one **theme** that is more important than any other in *Of Mice and Men*? Ask yourself which of the themes listed above, or any others you can think of, will stay longest in your memory.

For a C grade: select a theme that you think is the most important, say why you think it is (number of times it is mentioned, how important it seems to various characters) and writing clearly and appropriately, illustrate the theme and back up your statement of it by quotation.

For an A grade: show you are aware of all the themes in the novel, and don't be afraid to say that you don't think there is one more important than the others – if you're able to argue it convincingly! Also, explain the wide range of ways that themes are conveyed – through events, **characters**, **symbols** and so on.

PART SIX: GRADE BOOSTER

Understanding the question

Questions in exams or controlled conditions often need **'decoding'**. Decoding the question helps to ensure that your answer will be relevant and refers to what you have been asked.

 ## UNDERSTAND EXAM LANGUAGE

Get used to exam and essay style language by looking at specimen questions and the words they use. For example:

Exam speak!	Means?	Example
'convey ideas'	*'get across a point to the reader'* Usually you have to say *'how'* this is done.	The sad description of the dead puppy might *convey* the idea of a hard life for innocent people in *Of Mice and Men* (see pp. 92–3).
'methods, techniques, ways'	The *'things'* the writer does – such as a powerful description, introducing a shocking event, how someone speaks, etc.	The writer might use the *method* of contrasting characters to show good and bad, e.g. Slim versus Curley (see pp. 70–1).
'present, represent'	1) present: *'the way in which things are told to us'* 2) represent: *'what those things might mean underneath'*	The writer *presents* the reader with descriptions of the bunk house. It could *represent* a family home, or perhaps even a prison (see p. 19).

 ## 'BREAK DOWN' THE QUESTION

Pick out the **key words** or phrases. For example:

> **Question:** How does Steinbeck use the **character of Candy** to **represent** the **idea of broken dreams** in the novel?

● The focus is on character (Candy) so you will need to talk about him, what he does, says and how he is described by Steinbeck and the other characters.

● The words **'represent** the **idea of broken dreams'** tell us this a question that is equally about one of the novel's themes, e.g. 'broken or failed dreams'.

What does this tell you?

Focus on Candy not on other characters, except for their relationships to him (i.e Candy shares George and Lennie's dream).

 ## KNOW YOUR LITERARY LANGUAGE!

When studying texts you will come across words such as 'theme', 'symbol', 'imagery', 'metaphor', etc. Some of these words could come up in the question you are asked. Make sure you know what they mean before you use them!

Planning your answer

It is vital that you **plan** your response to the controlled assessment task or possible exam question carefully, and that you then follow your plan, if you are to gain the higher grades.

 ## DO THE RESEARCH!

When revising for the exam, or planning your response to the controlled assessment task, collect **evidence** (for example, quotations) that will support what you have to say. For example, if preparing to answer a question on how Steinbeck has explored the theme of loneliness, you might list ideas as follows:

Key point	Evidence/quotation	Page/chapter. etc
Loneliness is a major theme in the novel	'Guys like us, that work on ranches, are the loneliest guys in the world.'	Pages 14–15

 ## PLAN FOR PARAGRAPHS

Use paragraphs to plan your answer. For example:

1 The first paragraph should **introduce** the **argument** you wish to make.
2 Then, jot down how the paragraphs that follow will **develop** this argument. Include **details**, **examples** and other possible **points of view**. Each paragraph is likely to deal with one point at a time.
3 **Sum up** your argument in the last paragraph.

For example, for the following task:

Question: How does Steinbeck present the character of Curley's wife. Comment on the language devices and techniques used.

Simple plan:

● Paragraph 1: *Introduction*, e.g. Curley's wife is presented as both a dangerous person and a victim of loneliness. She is both guilty and innocent.

● Paragraph 2: *First point*, e.g. Steinbeck forewarns the reader by having Candy warn George about Curley's wife. Refer to Candy's first meeting with George.

● Paragraph 3: *Second point*, e.g. Steinbeck describes her in physical terms that emphasise her sexual attractiveness and her use of this to tease men.

● Paragraph 4: *Third point*, e.g. Curley's wife can be cruel, and willing to misuse power. Refer to what happens when she visits Crooks's room.

● Paragraph 5: *Fourth point,* e.g. She is also shown as vulnerable and a victim. Refer to the final description of her lying dead in the stable.

● Paragraph 6: *Conclusion*, e.g. Make sure to mention the comments Steinbeck made to the actress chosen to play Curley's wife.

How to use quotations

One of the secrets of success in writing essays is to use quotations **effectively**. There are five basic principles:

❶ Put quotation marks, e.g. ' ' around the quotation.

❷ Write the quotation exactly as it appears in the original.

❸ Do not use a quotation that repeats what you have just written.

❹ Use the quotation so that it fits into your sentence, or if it is longer indent it as a separate paragraph.

❺ Only quote what is most useful.

 **USE QUOTATIONS TO DEVELOP YOUR ARGUMENT**

Quotations should be used to develop the line of thought in your essays. Your comment should not duplicate what is in your quotation. For example:

GRADE D/E	GRADE C
(simply repeats the idea)	(makes a point and supports it with a relevant quotation)
Candy tells George that Curley is always picking fights with bigger men, as if Curley was angry that he was not bigger: 'He's alla time picking scraps with big guys. Kind of like he's mad at 'em because he ain't a big guy.' (p. 29)	Candy tells George that Curley is always picking fights with bigger men 'Kind of like he's mad at 'em because he ain't a big guy.' (p. 29)

However, the most sophisticated way of using the writer's words is to embed them into your sentence, and further develop the point:

GRADE A

(makes point, embeds quote and develops idea)

Candy tells George that Curley is 'alla time picking scraps with big guys', and that perhaps the reason is that 'he's mad at 'em because he ain't a big guy' (p. 29). In this way, Steinbeck conveys the idea of Curley seeming to be angry at the whole world, and permanently on the edge, looking for trouble.

When you use quotations in this way, you are demonstrating the ability to use text as evidence to support your ideas – not simply including words from the original to prove you have read it.

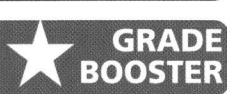 **EXAMINER'S TIP**

Try using a quotation to begin your response. You can use it as a launch pad for your ideas, or as an idea you are going to argue against.

GRADE BOOSTER

Where appropriate, refer to the language technique used by the writer and the effect it creates. For example, if you say, 'this metaphor shows how ...', or 'the effect of this metaphor is to emphasise to the reader ...' this could get you higher marks.

Sitting the examination

xamination papers are carefully designed to give you the opportunity to do your est. Follow these handy hints for exam success.

 BEFORE YOU START

- Make sure that you **know the texts** you are writing about so that you are properly prepared and equipped.

- You need to be **comfortable** and **free from distractions**. Inform the invigilator if anything is off-putting, e.g. a shaky desk.

- **Read** and follow the instructions, or rubric, on the front of the examination paper. You should know by now what you need to do but **check** to reassure yourself.

- Before beginning your answer have a **skim** through the **whole paper** to make sure you don't miss anything **importan**t.

- Observe the **time allocation** – and follow it carefully. If they recommend 45 minutes for a particular question on a text, make sure this is how long you spend.

EXAMINER'S TIP

Remember that you can say what you like – provided you have evidence for it from the book!

 WRITING YOUR RESPONSES

A typical 45 minute examination essay is probably between 550 and 800 words in length.

Ideally, spend a minimum of 5 minutes planning your answer before you begin.

Use the questions to structure your response. Here is an example:

Question: Do you see the ending of the novel as negative or positive? What methods does the writer use to lead you to this view?

- The introduction to your answer could briefly describe **the ending** of the novel.

- The second part could explain what could be seen as **positive**.

- The third part could be an exploration of the **negative** aspects.

- The conclusion would **sum up your own viewpoint**.

For each part allocate paragraphs to cover the points you wish to make (see **Planning your answer**).

Keep your writing clear and easy to read, using paragraphs and link words to show the structure of your answers.

Spend a couple of minutes afterwards quickly checking for obvious errors.

 'KEY WORDS' ARE THE KEY!

Keep on mentioning the **key words** from the question in your answer. This will keep you on track *and* remind the examiner that you are answering the question set.

Sitting the controlled assessment

It may be the case that you are responding to *Of Mice and Men* in a controlled assessment situation. Follow these useful tips for success.

 ## WHAT YOU ARE REQUIRED TO DO

Make sure you are clear about:

- The **specific text** and **task** you are preparing (is it just *Of Mice and Men*, or more than one text?).

- How **long** you have during the assessment period (i.e. 3–4 hours?).

- How **much** you are expected or allowed to write (i.e. 2,000 words?).

- **What** you are **allowed to take** into the controlled assessment, and what you can use (or not, as the case may be!). You may be able to take in brief notes but **not** draft answers, so check with your teacher.

 ## HOW YOU CAN PREPARE

Once you know your task, topic and text/s you can:

- Make **notes** and **prepare** the **points**, **evidence**, **quotations**, etc. you are likely to use.

- Practise or draft **model answers**.

- Use these **York Notes** to hone your **skills**, e.g. use of quotations, how to plan an answer and focus on what makes a **top grade**.

 ## DURING THE CONTROLLED ASSESSMENT

Remember:

- **Stick** to the topic and task you have been given.

- The allocated **time** is for **writing**, so make the most of it. It is double the time you might have in an exam, so you will be writing almost **twice as much** (or more).

- **If** you are **allowed** access to a **dictionary or thesaurus** make use of them; if not, don't go near them!

- At the end of the controlled assessment follow your **teacher's instructions**. For example, make sure you have written your **name** clearly on all the pages you hand in.

EXAMINER'S TIP

Don't just summarise the plot in your answer. The examiners know what happens in the book: they've read it too! Use the events of the novel to prove your point. Don't make those events your only point.

Improve your grade

is useful to know the type of responses examiners are looking for when they
ward different grades. The following broad guidance should help you to improve
our grade when responding to the task you are set!

GRADE C

What you need to show	What this means
Sustained response to task and text	You write enough! You don't run out of ideas after two paragraphs.
Effective use of **details** to **support** your **explanations**	You generally support what you say with evidence, e.g. *Crooks is treated badly by Curley's wife. Once she realises he disapproves of her, she threatens him, forcing him to back down in Section Four.*
Explanation of the writer's **use of language, structure, form**, etc., and the **effect on readers**	You must write about the writer's use of these things. It's not enough simply to give a viewpoint. So, you might comment on the way Steinbeck builds tension and suspense for the readers through small details, e.g. how the men play cards while waiting for Candy's dog to be shot, or how **similes** such as 'snorting … like a horse' are used to describe Lennie, as a sort of animal/beast.
Appropriate comment on **characters, plot, themes, ideas** and **settings**	Make sure what you say is relevant. If the task asks you to comment on how Crooks is treated, that is what you should write about.

GRADE A

What you need to show in addition to the above	What this means
Insightful, exploratory response to the text	You look beyond the obvious. You might question the idea of Lennie as a victim and say he deserved his fate; or, you might find some new aspect to comment on, e.g. how the setting of the ranch could be seen as a sort of prison. These need not be ideas you are sure about, but you can suggest them for the examiner to consider.
Close analysis and use of **detail**	If you are looking at the writer's use of language, you comment on each word in a sentence, drawing out its distinctive effect on the reader, e.g. when Curley's wife confides in Lennie, 'her words tumbled out in a passion of communication'. Here you might focus on how 'tumbled' suggests she is brimming with things she has to say, and 'passion' further emphasises her fiery and impulsive nature.
Convincing and **imaginative interpretation**	Your viewpoint is convincing to the examiner. You show you have engaged with the text, and come up with your own ideas. These may be based on what you have discussed in class or read about, but you have made your own decisions.

Annotated sample answers

This section will provide you with **extracts** from two **model answers**, one at **C grade** and one at **A grade**, to give you an idea of what is required to achieve at different levels.

Question: Read from page 36 ('A tall man stood in the doorway ...') to page 38 ('It's a lot nicer to go around with a guy you know'). Answer both parts of the question:

A   How do the details in the passage add to your understanding of Slim?

B   How does Steinbeck use the character of Slim in the novel as a whole to convey ideas about working life on ranches in 1930s America?

CANDIDATE 1

Says what the passage does

Interprets what the author is doing

Right to move to the second part of the question

Better – focusing on the working life now

Good supporting quote

John Steinbeck introduces Slim for the first time in this passage and we are shown what he looks like and how he behaves. It says that he was a 'tall man' and 'like the others, he wore blue jeans and a short denim jacket.' This means that he isn't trying to show off but is like the other men who work on the ranch. It also says that he has 'majesty'. This suggests that he is like the king of the ranch who everybody obeys or looks up to. Later when he sees George and Lennie, it says that he spoke 'kindly' and that his voice was 'gentle'.

In the novel as a whole Slim is important because he comes across as a kinder character who understands George and Lennie and sees that Lennie is a nice person really. But it shows also that working on a ranch is a hard life. Slim may be nice but he drowns the puppies when he has to. 'I drowned four of 'em right off. She couldn't feed that many.' He also agrees with Carlson shooting Candy's dog.

The most important thing, though, is that everyone respects Slim. Even Curley, who thinks Slim may be having an affair with his wife, is scared of him. 'Well, I didn't mean nothing, Slim. I justa ast you.' This is interesting because jobs are not easy to get in America in the 30s.

Correctly focuses on this passage

This quotation is good but it doesn't say what this adds

Weak description doesn't say much

Good – shows knowledge of social background

Overall comment: This is a solid response in which the student supports his/her views with some well-chosen quotations. Occasionally, the points made are not supported by evidence, and whilst the answer is clear and well argued, there is not very much evidence of original, or alternative thinking. Perhaps more reference to Slim's majestic approach and understanding would also help.

GRADE C

CANDIDATE 2

riginal thought
nking Slim to
lm

ery well-chosen
uotation with
xplanation

gain, inventive
ea to think of
im as feminine

ts of supporting
ferences but no
uotes

teresting
ntrast with
urley and widens
ut to mention the
ook as a 'tragedy'

> The introduction of Slim into the novel could almost be the introduction of a hero from a classic Western as he 'stood in the doorway', as if framed in a film. And this idea is developed as the passage goes on, with his skill as a 'jerkline skinner' emphasised by his ability to kill flies with a 'bull whip without touching the mule.'
>
> More importantly, his skills extend beyond his work; he is clearly respected and listened to – 'his word was taken on any subject, be it politics or love', and the description of his hands which are 'delicate as those of a temple dancer' make him sound almost feminine despite their being 'large and lean'.
>
> What this passage shows, then, is that an ordinary working man, who shares a room in a bunk house, can have 'majesty' and 'gravity' – and, through the use of the word 'kindly', shows he understands Lennie and George.
>
> Nevertheless, although our initial impressions of Slim are positive, we should not be blind to the fact that the ranch life is a tough life; Slim is forced to drown four puppies because the mother wouldn't have enough to feed them, and he allows Carlson to shoot Candy's dog. Even he doesn't stand in the way of Lennie being killed. This is a tough society in which people take the law into their own hands – as Lennie and George found out when they were in Weed.
>
> In addition, although Slim is presented by Steinbeck as intelligent, perceptive and a skilled worker, it has not brought him particular success. He is still a worker who lives in the bunk house, and is as likely to face being fired as much as anyone else. He, unlike George, doesn't appear to have friends as such – and is therefore isolated.
>
> Though, Slim reminds us that for every Curley – unpleasant, rich, and violent – there are decent, honourable characters and although the book could be seen as a sort of tragedy of American life, it ends with Slim comforting George after he kills Lennie. 'You hadda George. I swear you hadda.'

Shows how the writer develops our understanding of Slim

Good – focusing on the working life now

Rather a weak quote to end but it does support the point

Overall comment: This is an outstanding response with few weak points. Quotations and evidence are woven skilfully into the answer, and there are several examples of original thinking and ideas. The response is slightly weaker in the second half with perhaps not enough reference to working life on the farm and Slim's place within it, but overall this is very successful.

GRADE A

Further questions

The following questions are a representative sample of examination questions from all the major examination boards.

EXAM-STYLE QUESTIONS

❶ Read the start of Section Three when George talks to Slim: what do you think first caused George and Lennie to travel as a pair, and why do they stay together?

❷ In what way are dreams an important theme in the novel, and why do you think George and Lennie are unable to achieve theirs?

❸ There are four main settings for the novel: the bunk house, the harness room, the barn and the pond. Choose one and write about why you think it is the most important.

❹ How is the character Curley important to the novel as a whole?

❺ What can we learn about the sort of life workers experienced during this time in the United States?

CONTROLLED ASSESSMENT-STYLE QUESTIONS

❻ How is the theme of friendship presented in the novel?

❼ Explore the way power is presented in the novel – to what extent is *Of Mice and Men* about people who abuse the power they have over each other?

❽ How does Steinbeck create a distinctive sense of voice in the novel through his use of speech and dialogue?

❾ Explore the way the relationship between Lennie and George is presented through focusing on particular language devices and techniques.

❿ In what ways can the views of the author be seen in the way the ideas and themes are presented?

Literary terms

Literary term	Explanation
Character(s)	Either a person in a play, novel, etc., or his or her personality.
Colloquial	The everyday speech used by people in ordinary situations.
Dialogue	A conversation between two or more characters, or the words spoken by characters in general.
Foreshadow	Where the author provids a hint of events to come – this could be through an image, a symbol or a conversation between characters.
Imagery	Descriptive language that uses images to make actions, objects and characters more vivid in the reader's mind. Metaphors and similes are examples of imagery.
Irony	When someone deliberately says one thing when they mean another, usually in a humorous or sarcastic way.
Metaphor	When one thing is used to describe another thing to create a striking or unusual image.
Motif	A repeated theme or idea.
Paradox	Where something outwardly contradictory is shown to be true.
Sarcasm	An extreme form of irony, usually intended to be hurtful.
Simile	When one thing is compared directly to another, using the word 'like' or 'as'.
Symbol(ism)	Where an object, person or a thing is used to represent another thing.
Theme	A central idea examined by an author.

Checkpoint answers

Checkpoint 1
Lizard, rabbits, racoon, dogs, deer, heron, mouse, water snake, carp, chickens.

Checkpoint 2
It is long, rectangular, whitewashed, with an unpainted floor, three windows and eight bunks. A box to serve as shelving is nailed over each bunk. There is a cast-iron stove and a long table.

Checkpoint 3
We know four people are there: Crooks, Lennie, Candy and Curley's wife. We don't know if the Boss is there.

Checkpoint 4
This is one of those issues where you can make your own mind up, showing the examiner that you have the capacity for original and independent thought.

Checkpoint 5
His face is compared to a hatchet, he drowns some of his dog's puppies, supports the shooting of Candy's dog and the shooting of Lennie. Yet he does not seem cruel, but rather practical and realistic.

Checkpoint 6
He shows concern about lice in his bunk and arranges his washing and shaving material carefully over his bunk.

Checkpoint 7
Probably not. Children are small, and learn more as they grow older. Lennie is huge, and will never learn more than he knows now.

Checkpoint 8
Shotgun, medicines, several pairs of shoes, rubber boots, alarm clock, books, magazines, spectacles.

Checkpoint 9
Probably not. Crooks and Candy are bitter, but Slim, Carlson and Whit seem perfectly happy.

Checkpoint 10
Between a third and a half of the novel is written in direct speech or **dialogue**. Steinbeck tells us what the characters look like, but lets them tell us in their own words what they think and feel.

Checkpoint 11
No. Some of the book's language is very much of its time, but the ideas and characters have a universal meaning and relevance.